Born with Purpose

Cecilia Rubio-Watkins

Illustrator Caleb Toilolo

Trilogy Christian Publishers
A Wholly Owned Subsidiary of Trinity Broadcasting Network
2442 Michelle Drive
Tustin, CA 92780

For information, address Trilogy Christian Publishing
Rights Department, 2442 Michelle Drive, Tustin, Ca 92780.
Trilogy Christian Publishing/ TBN and colophon are trademarks of Trinity Broadcasting Network.

For information about special discounts for bulk purchases, please contact Trilogy Christian Publishing.

Manufactured in the United States of America

10 9 8 7 6 5 4 3 2 1

Library of Congress Cataloging-in-Publication Data is available.

ISBN 978-1-64773-762-7 (Print Book)
ISBN 978-1-64773-763-4 (ebook)

This book is dedicated to every generation. The words of this book are inspired by the Word of God. It is our hope that you and your children would know who God created you to be. Enjoy.

Foreword

"As a parent of two children under 5, this book is a great introduction to who God created them to be before they entered the world. Sit down with your kids for a great bed time impartation and get growing."

Michael Watkins

Introduction

Father, in the name of Jesus, I ask that you give each reader eyes to see and ears to hear what the Spirit of the Lord is saying for their individual purpose. Direct and guide them through the gift of life. We thank You for life and life abundantly over the reader and their families. Amen.

Before I was born, the Lord saved me and called
me into existence. He formed me while I was still
in my mommy's womb (see Isaiah 44:24 ICB).

2

I am unique and unlike anyone else.
The Lord created me. He made my mind and heart;
He wove me together in my mommy's womb.
(see Psalm 139:13 ICB)

4

From the very beginning of time, God made all humans in His likeness. He made me just the same.

He created male and female, blessed us, and named us humans (see Genesis 5:2-3 ICB).

5

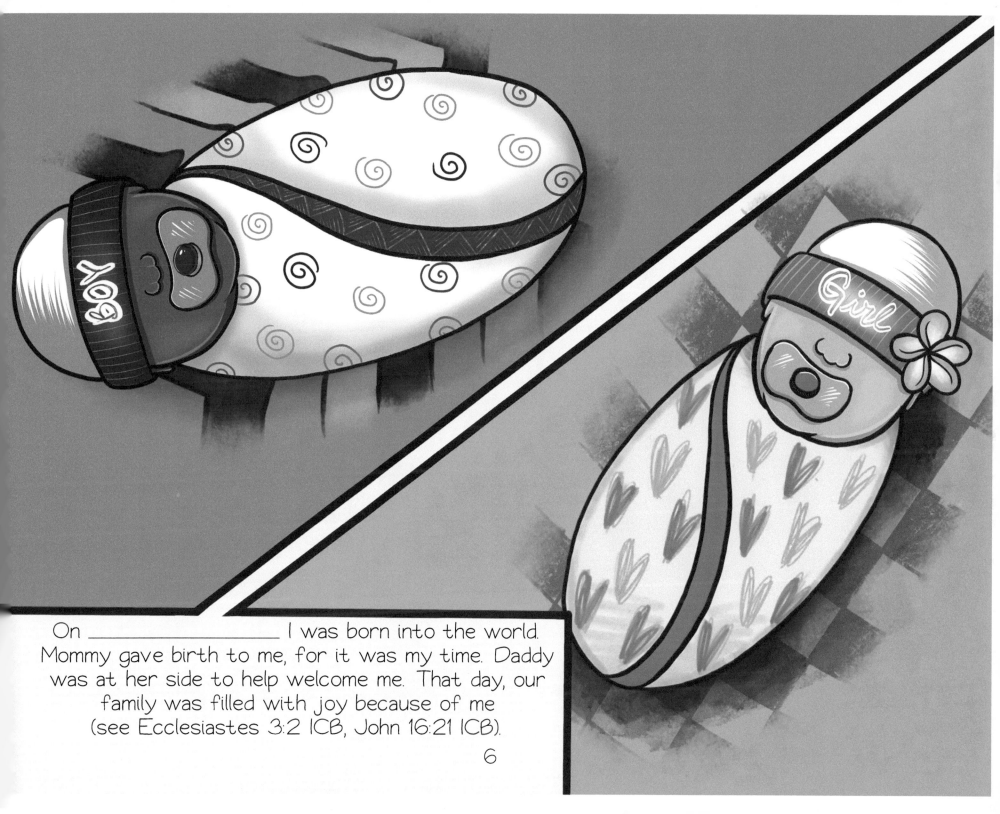

On _____ I was born into the world.
Mommy gave birth to me, for it was my time. Daddy
was at her side to help welcome me. That day, our
family was filled with joy because of me
(see Ecclesiastes 3:2 ICB, John 16:21 ICB).

6

Mommy and Daddy are my teachers; they show me how to live. They show me how to love and be kind and what is right and wrong, so when I'm big, I will live the life God purposed for me (see Proverbs 22:6 ICB).

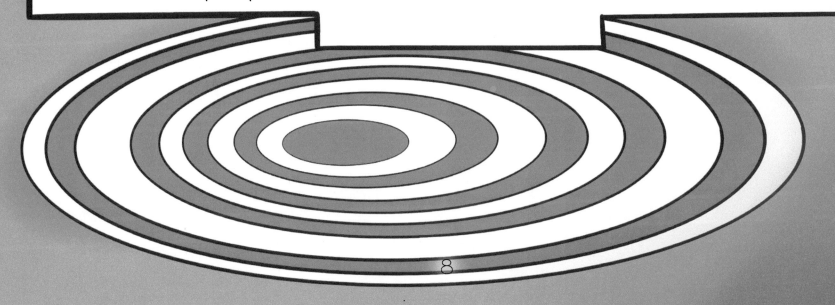

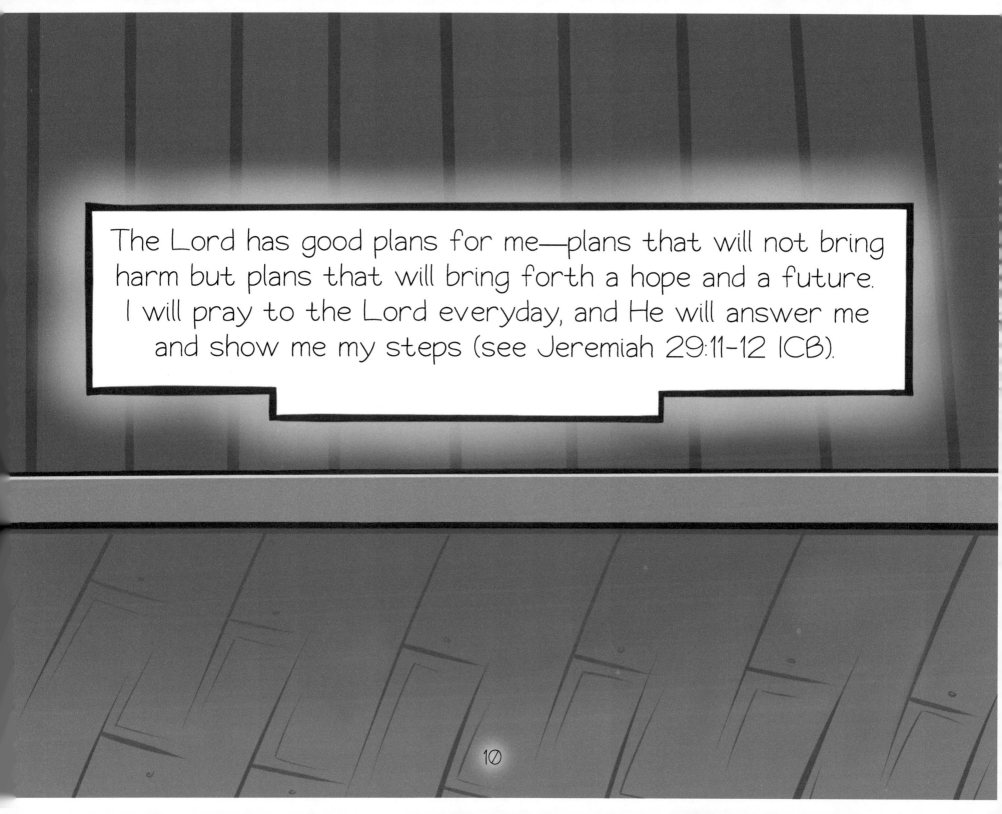

The Lord has good plans for me—plans that will not bring harm but plans that will bring forth a hope and a future. I will pray to the Lord everyday, and He will answer me and show me my steps (see Jeremiah 29:11-12 ICB).

Great is my purpose and mighty are my deeds God has planned for me. My eyes are open to the way of all humans. I am rewarded daily as I live out this promise (see Jeremiah 32:19 ICB and NASB).

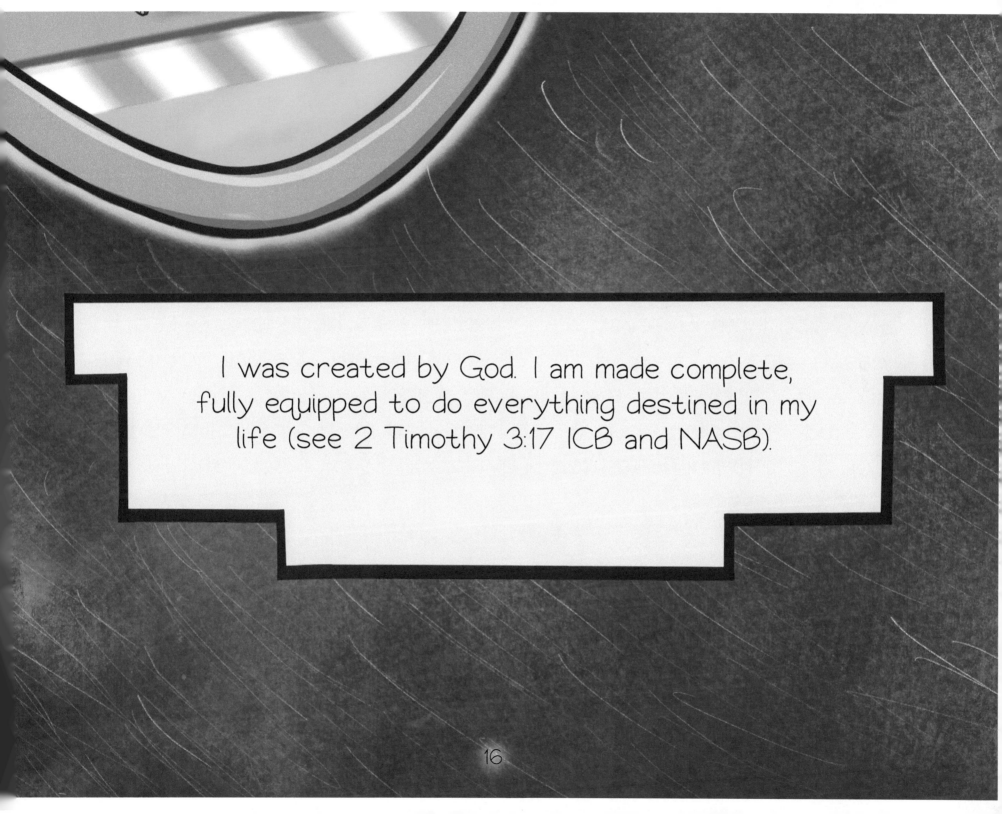

I was created by God. I am made complete, fully equipped to do everything destined in my life (see 2 Timothy 3:17 ICB and NASB).

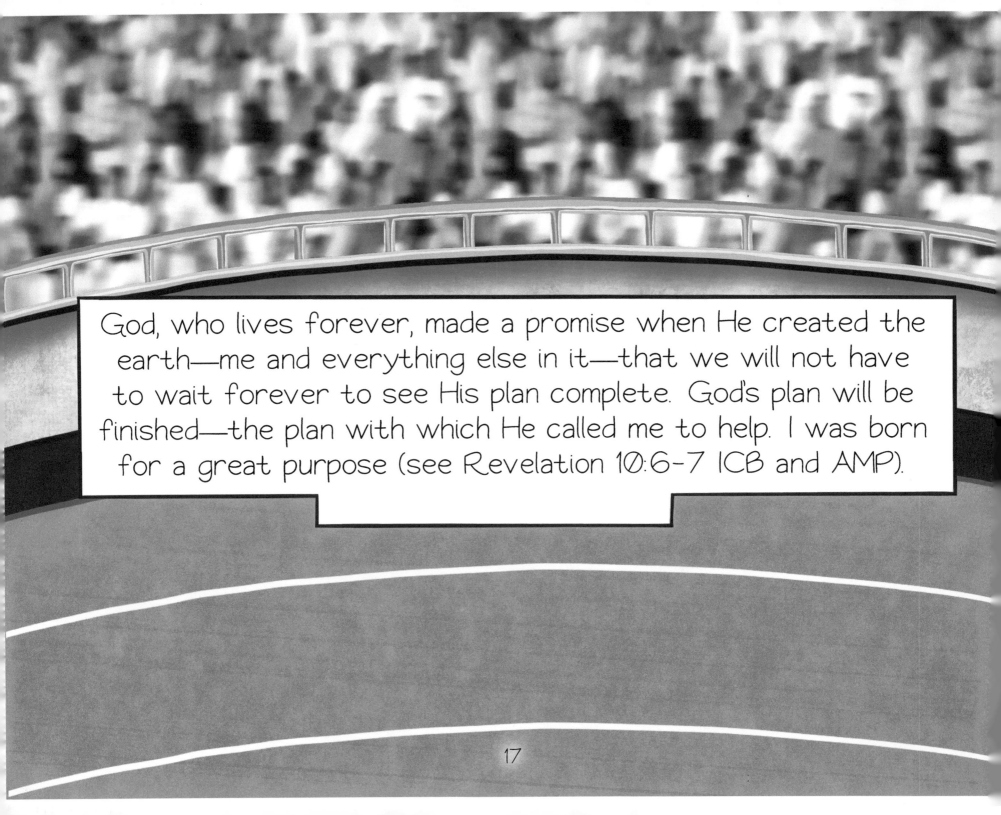

God, who lives forever, made a promise when He created the earth—me and everything else in it—that we will not have to wait forever to see His plan complete. God's plan will be finished—the plan with which He called me to help. I was born for a great purpose (see Revelation 10:6-7 ICB and AMP).

Daily Declaration

God, I declare the purpose You saw in me and saved me for will be what leads me in life. I declare that I will listen and obey my parents' teachings, for it will help guide me to my future. I declare that, as I pursue the desires of my heart, placed there by You, that I will see all truth in humans around me. I declare that my purpose will be seen through the eyes of those I meet. I declare You are preparing every next step before I get there because You love me. I declare I will rejoice with You when the plan is complete (see Job 22:28 AMP and NASB).

CPSIA information can be obtained
at www.ICGtesting.com
Printed in the USA
BVHW092006020321
601491BV00016B/184